Chien-Shiung Wu

Jennifer Strand

abdopublishing.com

Published by Abdo Zoom™, PO Box 398166, Minneapolis, Minnesota 55439. Copyright © 2017 by Abdo Consulting Group, Inc. International copyrights reserved in all countries. No part of this book may be reproduced in any form without written permission from the publisher. Abdo Zoom™ is a trademark and logo of Abdo Consulting Group, Inc.

Printed in the United States of America, North Mankato, Minnesota
102016
012017

Cover Photo: Gjon Mili/The LIFE Picture Collection/Getty Images
Interior Photos: Gjon Mili/The LIFE Picture Collection/Getty Images, 1; Bettmann/Getty Images, 5, 10; SPL/Science Source, 6; Science Source, 8, 9, 13, 15, 18–19; Everett Historical/Shutterstock Images, 11; AP Images, 14; Robert W. Kelley/The LIFE Picture Collection/Getty Images, 16; James Burke/The LIFE Picture Collection/Getty Images, 17

Editor: Brienna Rossiter
Series Designer: Madeline Berger
Art Direction: Dorothy Toth

Publisher's Cataloging-in-Publication Data
Names: Strand, Jennifer, author.
Title: Chien-shiung Wu / by Jennifer Strand.
Description: Minneapolis, MN : Abdo Zoom, 2017. | Series: Technology pioneers
    | Includes bibliographical references and index.
Identifiers: LCCN 2016948917 | ISBN 9781680799286 (lib. bdg.) |
    ISBN 9781624025143 (ebook) | 9781624025709 (Read-to-me ebook)
Subjects: LCSH: Wu, C.S.(Chien-shiung), 1912-1997--Juvenile literature. |
    Nuclear physicists--United States--Biography--Juvenile literature. | Nuclear
    physicists--China--Biography--Juvenile literature. | Women physicists--
    Biography--Juvenile literature. | Chinese Americans--Biography--Juvenile
    literature.
Classification: DDC 530.92 [B]--dc23
LC record available at http://lccn.loc.gov/2016948917

Table of Contents

Introduction

Chien-Shiung Wu was a respected scientist. She was from China. She studied **physics** and **radioactivity**.

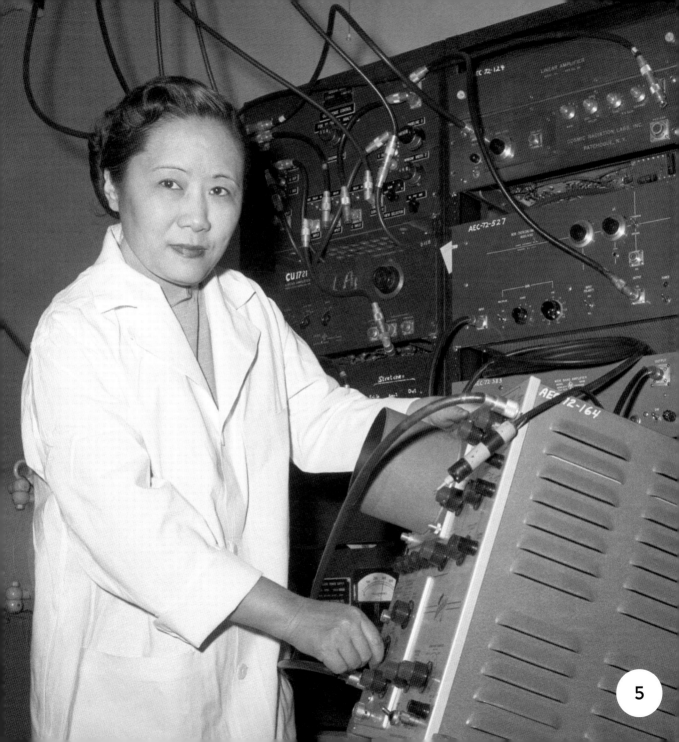

Early Life

Chien-Shiung was born on May 31, 1912. She loved to read.

Many girls in
China could not
go to school. But
Chien-Shiung wanted
to study physics.
She worked
very hard.

Wu became a college professor.

She went to the United States to study more. She learned from great scientists. She did **research**, too.

9

Wu helped scientists learn how to make fuel for atomic bombs.

The bombs helped end
World War II (1939–1945).

Two scientists asked Wu for help. They wanted to test a law of physics. Wu did **experiments**. She proved that their ideas were correct.

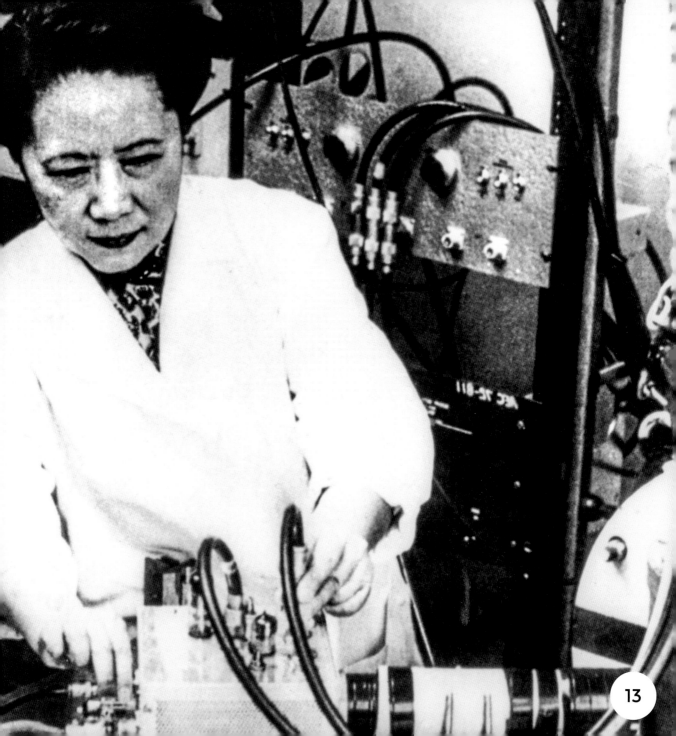

The two scientists won a **Nobel Prize**. Wu did not, even though she worked with them.

But she kept doing research.

Wu won many awards.
She worked to help
women in science.

16

She traveled and gave advice to scientists, too.

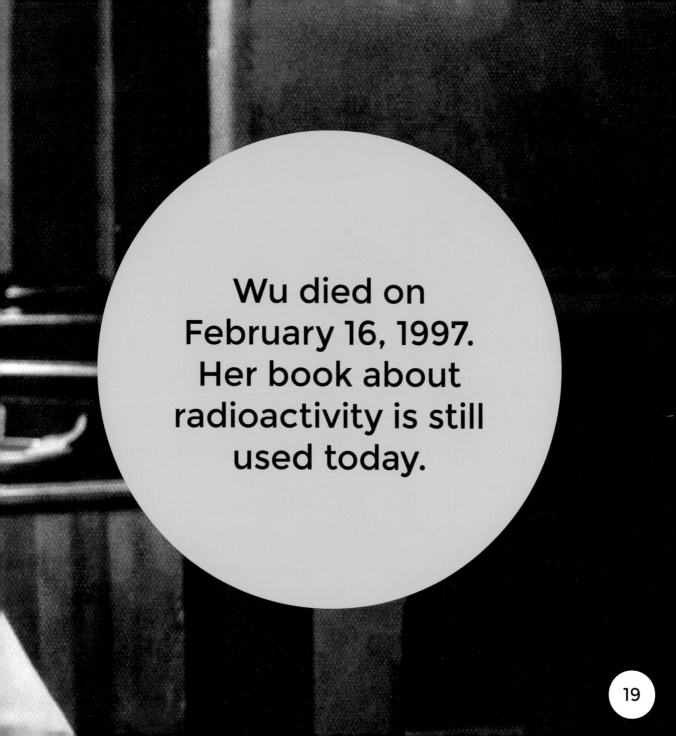

Wu died on February 16, 1997. Her book about radioactivity is still used today.

Chien-Shiung Wu

Born: May 31, 1912

Birthplace: Liuhe, China

Husband: Luke Chia-Liu Yuan

Known For: Wu was a scientist. She studied physics and radioactivity. Her research won many awards.

Died: February 16, 1997

Key Dates

1912: Chien-Shiung Wu is born on May 31.

1944: Wu joins the top-secret Manhattan Project to help develop an atomic bomb.

1946: Wu starts to do research about beta decay.

1956: Wu proves that the law of parity does not always apply.

1975: President Gerald Ford gives Wu the National Medal of Science.

1997: Wu dies on February 16.

Glossary

experiment - a scientific test.

Nobel Prize - an important award given out each year.

physics - the science that deals with matter, energy, motion, and force.

radioactivity - the tiny particles that are given off when atoms break apart.

research - careful study that is done to learn new facts or to solve a problem.

Booklinks

For more information
on **Chien-Shiung Wu**, please visit
booklinks.abdopublishing.com

Zoom In on Biographies!

Learn even more with the Abdo Zoom
Biographies database. Check out
abdozoom.com for more information.

Index